IN RELATION TO THE WHOLE

RACKSTRAW DOWNES

RACKSTRAW DOWNES

In Relation to the Whole
THREE ESSAYS FROM THREE DECADES
1973, 1981, 1996

EDGEWISE
New York - Paris - Turin
24 FIFTH AVENUE, N° 224
2000

THE FIRST FIFTY COPIES
OF THIS EDITION
ARE SIGNED AND NUMBERED
BY THE AUTHOR:

/50

IN RELATION TO THE WHOLE:
THREE ESSAYS FROM THREE DECADES – 1973, 1981, 1996
by Rackstraw Downes.
Copyright © 2000 Rackstraw Downes.
All Rights Reserved.
Published by Edgewise Press, Inc.
New York - Paris - Turin.
Edgewise Press: 24 Fifth Avenue, N° 224, New York, N.Y. 10011.
First Edition, April 2000.
Library of Congress Catalog Card Number: 98-074409.
I.S.B.N.: 1-893207-03-X.
Printed by Dal Broi Servizi Grafico Editoriali, s.a.s., Turin, Italy.
Frontispiece photograph of the author by Jed Devine.

CONTENTS

9 *Preface*

11 What the Sixties Meant to Me (1973)

33 What Realism Means to Me (1981)

53 The Tenses of Landscape (1996)

PREFACE

You and the culture evolve differently. It seems stuck while you feel restless, or it gets restless when you, like a broody hen, need to keep faith. But, as with the 'stiff twin compasses' of Donne's poem, the dynamic between the two of you is unavoidably connective, no matter how close or far apart you get. You address this variable distance. Finding yourself from time to time in a different place, you write from there.

That's how it is with the three essays selected here. Each deals with some concern of a different decade. In the 1960s it was impossible to pick the mentors I did, to write what I wrote or paint what I painted without defiance — the art world by and large had not been listening. In the 1970s this changed; realism got attention — a moment to write about it with a sense of its amplitude, its resonance and implications. By the 1980s all iconography was considered political: the 'landscape' became the 'environment'. This was not all wrong, but the oversimplifications and polarizations were antithetical to the thoughtful art I wanted.

These pieces were all written on invitation, as talks. One is printed here for the first time, the others have been left, except for printers' errors, pretty much as they were.

R.D.

WHAT THE SIXTIES MEANT TO ME (1973)

Metaphor, for example, marks in its naive principle a groping, a hesitation between several different expressions of one thought, an explosive incapacity that surpasses the necessary and sufficient capacity. Once one has gone over and made the thought rigorously precise, restricted it to a single object, then the metaphor will be effaced, and prose will reappear.

— Paul Valéry

I

The subject of art is life. Works of art are metaphors of life. A statement is the vehicle for a thought, discarded as soon as the thought is communicated; a simile is an illustration to such a statement. But a metaphor is unique, inexhaustible and untranslatable; there is no other way to say it. Metaphors are necessary to life as an illumination of it; as Shakespeare said, "Art holds the mirror up to nature," and it is in the mirror that we come to know ourselves. So that, though art may be amusing, it is not an amusement. But art's metaphors may cease to exist. If the mystery of life is explained and a science of its functionings perfected, there would be no need of art. An alliance, for example, between social scientists, behavioral psychologists, and genetic engineers could achieve this. Then we can all move to Levittown, raise 2.1 children per couple, and play 10 holes of golf on Saturday morning. This was Blake's idea of Hell: "The Bible says That Cultivated Life Existed First. Uncultivated Life comes afterwards from Satan's Hirelings. Necessaries, Accommodations & Ornaments are the whole of Life. Satan took away Ornament

First. Next he took away Accommodations, & Then he became Lord & Master of Necessaries." The triumvirate I imagine aims to perfect a system of the Necessaries. Is this why artists are frequently Tories? Do not the southern senators lead the opposition to a centralized, computerized Data Bank?

In Jean Renoir's film *Boudu Saved from Drowning* the tramp Boudu throws himself into the Seine and a crowd of onlookers assembles. A middle-class bookseller feels it is his social responsibility to save and house him. Far from being grateful, Boudu is merely irritated to find himself saved and enjoys creating anarchic mayhem in his benefactor's household. Boudu and the bookseller are metaphors of art and society. The mirror that reveals us to ourselves both fascinates and frightens: so the bookseller is both intrigued and infuriated by the disruptive Boudu. To save a tramp promises self-esteem and the applause of his neighbors; but in fact Boudu subverts the structure, and clumsily uncovers the little hypocrisies of the bookseller's mode of life. Boudu in turn is tempted: society almost tames him and marries him off to the maid — he rather fancies himself as a bridegroom and lords it up at the well-provided wedding picnic. But he finally slips away from such comforts and constraints, trades his nicely tailored clothes with those of a scarecrow, and returns to the life of a hungry but free-wheeling vagabond. He cannot quite make the compromise with a world that would force him to be untrue to his own nature.

Utopians from Plato to Mondrian have realized that it is art's uselessness to society, the impossibility of fitting it in, that would unsettle their schemes for a perfect, regulated humanity. Plato wished to banish the poets. The declared aim of Mondrian was to use his art to dispense with art itself.

WHAT THE SIXTIES MEANT TO ME

He considered his paintings as sketches for the design of an urban Utopia in which there would be no more pictures. He argued that the absolutes of the vertical/horizontal relationship and primary colors are conducive to stability, and would eliminate tragedy (and, one might add, joy also, since there is no light without shade nor shade without light). But it is probable, as E.M. Forster predicted in his story "The Machine Stops," that in a Utopia someone possessed of the vitality that characterizes human life would feel compelled to qualify or destroy the stasis that would obtain there. Such a person would be an artist.

Art used to be the more or less exclusive prerogative of the church and the aristocracy, institutions which guaranteed their members a security based on orders — hereditary or divine — that were greater than the individuals themselves. So that if art disturbed them it could not destroy them. Even the greatest art did not cower them, for their position suggested that they were above it. So Pope Paul IV was not ashamed to say of Michelangelo's *Last Judgment* that it was better suited to a bath house than a holy place. (El Greco offered his services to replace the whole fresco with one "modest and decent and no less well-painted than the other.") But in the middle of the eighteenth century when Voltaire had undermined the church and the forces of the French and American Revolutions were toppling the institutions of the aristocracy, the bourgeoisie began to patronize the arts at the great French Salons. The middle classes are socially the most insecure of all, neither hopeless underdogs like peasants, nor sustained by family trees like aristocrats, nor validated by God, as prelates are. Valéry pointed out that Insurance and Contraception, those personifications of caution, were both invented by the bourgeoisie. As the middle classes wandered through the confusing variety of the salons, they wanted to be sure about what was good. It was then that modern art criticism was born.

It was the job of the critic to judge, and to justify his judgments. For instance Diderot, who might be called the first modern art critic, admired the subject pictures of Greuze because they taught a moral lesson. But it is obvious that you can have the moral lesson without the work of art itself, so this was not adequate as a justification for art. In our century criticism has found another rationale for what is good in art. It borrowed it from the nineteenth-century philosopher Hegel. He thought that by examining the past you could detect trends or movements on the basis of which you could scientifically predict the future. Marx, who as a young man was very interested in Hegel's idea, thought that you could and should implement your prediction. This led to a new kind of intellectual who not only wrote about tendencies in the past or present, but felt he could predict and direct the future: in the guise of an art critic his message to the artist was: since I know where art is going you'll be all washed up if you don't go that way too.

The art historian has for many years been devoting much of his energy to characterizing large general movements in the art of the past by which he connects one discreet object to another. It is easy to see how well this historical method plays into the hands of the Marxist art critic; operating somewhere between the historian and the artist he is in the perfect position to play controller and fit art into a consolingly explicable pattern or plan. Interpreting the historian's knowledge of the past he can tell artists what they ought to do next; or he can inspect a new work and say, Does this or does this not further art history, and if it does not it is no longer good art. So it was that when de Kooning painted his Women the critic Clement Greenberg walked up to him in the Cedar Bar and said "You're dead." This critic thought that art had been getting more and more pure since 1860 and should no longer have images or space. De Kooning was not dead of course. But from then on in the minds of many people his day was over and it was time to turn the spotlight on artists who were getting on with history. This preoccupation of art with history became so obsessive that not long afterwards Saul Steinberg said "We now have art historical art being made by art historical artists for art historians." Quite a few artists had figured out that they could make a career out of illustrating art history.

By the 1960s American art, which had been considered an unimportant suburb of Paris, had become, through the work of the Abstract Expressionists, world-famous. Prices went up. The 1960s were an inflationary decade in general. To invest in such expensive art, museum directors and collectors wanted some guarantee on their purchases; a place in history was the best possible surety. So they liked a kind of criticism which suggested that you could tell straight away what was going to be in history and what was not. Thus, based on the supposed purification of art since 1860 we were given the pure art of color field painting, the purer art of Minimal painting and sculpture, and finally the purest art of all, just the idea without the object, Conceptual art.

But the vocabulary of historical method is not limited to continuation; it permits reaction too. The proponents of Pop art thought they had just as good a case as the proponents of pure art: for Pop was a reaction to what was considered "the" historical style of the 1950s, Abstract Expressionism. This style had been abstract, highbrow, difficult, soul-searching, and hermetic. The images of Pop were recognizable, familiar, maybe even funny, sassy, vulgar; and it was done by artists who had had a commercial training in many cases, so it also looked manually skillful. This was reassuring after the messy Abstract Expressionist pictures which some people thought monkeys could have painted just as well. The audience for Pop was therefore huge, and the art world took on the aspect of a giddy and glamorous party.

These manifestations constituted the official Salon art of the 1960s. They had an aggressive critical literature, and their public relations were highly developed. Whereas the 1950s had been years of cooperatively owned and operated galleries and of comparatively modest dealers who leaned on the advice of their artists, the monied '60s saw the development of an extensive, high-powered management of critics, impresarios, dealers, and curators whose idea appeared to be to stage a stylistic "advance" for every season. The work in each one-man show began to look all alike so you could distinguish at a glance who was doing what — just like the divisions of labor in the old French salons. Old galleries got a face lift, new galleries looked prosperous and sleek. Whatever the merits of this art may eventually appear to have been, it — and the world which surrounded it — was not for me. The money in collusion with an officialdom of tastemakers, the arguable and, in any event, inconsequential theoretical basis of it, and the narrow specialization of the artists created an atmosphere in which art as I understood it could hardly breathe. Considering the parallel public events — B.F. Skinner's totalitarian behavioralism, Marshall McLuhan's gaga technological euphoria, and last but not least, the war in Vietnam, it was a decade that could hardly have ended soon enough for me.

II

To see this, the official art of the 1960s, you tramped Madison Avenue beginning at Emmerich and ending with Castelli. But there was another route which some people took; it included Frumkin, de Nagy, Zabriskie, Schoelkopf, Peridot, Graham among others. In these galleries one saw an art which looked awkwardly inexplicable; like so much of the liveliest art of any time it eluded critical dialectic. By the official art world it was virtually dismissed. And so I would call it the "unofficial" art of the 1960s. This was the world which interested me. It was the only art of quality that did not seem stage-managed; it had no party platform, no campaign. It did not bully you into believing it was "right," a condition impossible to art and which, when claimed by a school or a critic, automatically makes the art seem slightly suspect. In contrast to the official styles these works looked to me like spontaneous facts of art, not calculated entries in the annals of history. Though this art had no critical polemic, it had a criticism; for the essays of Fairfield Porter on Class Consciousness in American Abstract Painting, on Art and Knowledge, on The Prendergast Anomaly, and on Joseph Cornell, constituted what I took and still take to be the most serious and profound criticism in those years. Porter seemed to be writing an Areopagitica for art, freeing it from its bureaucrats, distinguishing it from ideas and ideals, from words, theories, and justifications: from professionalism, from social service, and from technology's separation of the thinking from the sensuous part of a person.

In 1964 John Bernard Myers, in an article called "Junkdump Fair Surveyed," called this art "private." And in a sense it was, for as I say it made no overtures to the critical continuum which mediates between the artist and his audience. But it was not intended to be kept private. It was exhibited; it had a small following of patrons, intellectuals, practitioners of other arts. Can it be more precisely characterized? Many of the pictures I speak of contained recognizable images, and for this reason they were often called "figurative." But this only served to distinguish it from nonfigurative art, to which it was not opposed, as abstract art tended to be opposed, on historicist grounds, to "figurative" art. Most of the artists of whom I speak had started out as abstract artists. Neither was it a "school" in the usual sense of that term; for the artists often disapproved of each other's work. In this sense they were moderns; that is to say, artists who do not share or observe an inherited body of knowledge, skills, or critical precepts, or specified aims. (It was Picasso who, I believe rightly, identified working in solitude and so sharing no goals, as the common denominator of the Post-Impressionists, the founders of modern art.) I think that the figurative element in this work was not an attempt to oppose abstract painting, but to enlarge and increase the resources of painting. Alex Katz has recorded that he was trying to paint the light coming through the trees, and that when he saw Pollock's work he realized that Pollock had painted that sensation. But Katz's paintings of that time make it clear that he wanted the light sensation *and* the recognizable trees too.

This desire for a more complete and inclusive art also led these painters to take a fresh look at the past masters; they were not, in the words of Coleridge, artists who wished "to destroy the wisdom of ages in order to substitute the fancies of a day." The issue was that they needed the past to help adapt and expand the means that abstract art had bequeathed them. From the Marxist point of view I suppose these artists looked like so many lily-livered Christopher Columbuses turning back in mid-Atlantic; but it was not timidity, but ambition, the hunger for a more complete language and more complicated undertakings, that led them to reinspect the past. Some of them would probably deny that this issue existed, some perhaps consciously tried to dodge it in their art; certainly none seemed to agree in the slightest about what to use from the past, or even what was good there. Each had to invent his own "tradition," his own version of art's aristocracy. I think it is significant that no European art to my knowledge has been quite so intrepid as some of these painters in the face of jeering accusations of "revivalism." For in Europe, where those traditions flourished most perfectly and fully, they are still, if weakly, in the bloodstream. Recent American painting, with the exception of a figure like Edwin Dickinson who maintains a contact with the trans-Atlantic tradition of Hawthorne and Chase, and an immigrant like Joseph Floch who was trained in Paris and remains a Continental painter, did not have that. Therefore the past was something to *discover*, as much of a frontier as California to a train of covered wagons. It had then the typically American attraction of starting from scratch. I recently revisited England and was talking to an old friend. It turned out that both of us had taken up gardening since we last met. She pulled out a catalogue of rare Tudor roses which she grows on a trellis on the wall of her seventeenth-century cottage. I had to explain that to me gardening meant tilling a little compost into the corner of an abandoned field and raising a few cucumbers and carrots.

In the Preface to his *Dictionary* Dr. Johnson wrote "So far have I been from any care to grace my pages with modern decorations, that I have studiously endeavoured to collect examples and authorities from the writers before the

Restoration, whose works I regarded as the 'wells of English undefiled,' as the pure sources of genuine diction.... From the authors which rose in the time of Elizabeth a speech might be formed adequate to all the purposes of use and elegance. If the language of theology were extracted from Hooker and the translation of the Bible; the terms of natural knowledge from Bacon; the phrases of policy, war, and navigation from Raleigh; the dialect of poetry and fiction from Spenser and Sidney; and the diction of common life from Shakespeare, few ideas would be lost to mankind, for want of English words in which they might be expressed." It was not that these painters thought of the art of the past as pure wells of painting undefiled, but rather as rich wells of painting unreduced.

It was this interest in the past, so blatant in some of the artists, that threw the critics, preoccupied with the shades of Marx and Hegel, the most. But had these critics kept their eye on the history of art rather than the theory of political history, they might have reacted a little differently. For art, all the arts, are constantly looking to the past for help and inspiration. Indeed the great inventors in music and literature as well as the plastic arts have *as a rule* been revivalists too. One thinks of Donatello and Brunelleschi measuring Roman antiquities, David drawing them all over again three centuries later, Cézanne haunting the museums and assiduously drawing there; in poetry, of Wordsworth and Coleridge immersed in Bishop Percy's *Reliques of the Old English Ballads*. Whenever art begins to feel boxed in, its norms and canons hardened, its criticism regulatory, it might be taken as commonplace that artists look to the past for help. Perhaps they seek precisely what the art of their own time lacks the most: for David, for example, Roman severity was the antithesis of the curvaceous Rococo. Some quite extreme, not to say desperate and bizarre manifestations of this kind have been known. In the middle of the eighteenth century some English poets felt such a distaste for the frozen norms of poetic diction and the heroic couplet (whose rhythms were so ingrained that even the blank verse of the time merely sounded like unrhymed couplets), and for the academically Aristotelian criticism of the time, that they could see no other way out but to write forgeries of Old English and Norse poems like the Rowley and Ossian poems of Chatterton and MacPherson. Public taste at the time seems to have been a little sharper than official taste, for the public adored them as they did the genuinely old ballads in Bishop Percy's Reliques. They were raw cries of passion in the claustrophobic teatime atmosphere of late eighteenth-century literature. In retrospect one sees that it was precisely these poems that heralded English romantic poetry, the art that led and best expressed the changing sensibility of Europe. Today, as we approach the last quarter of the twentieth century, we have hardly yet unshackled ourselves from concepts (expressed in code words like "avant-garde," "advanced," and "mainstream") which are in fact the orphaned offspring of mid-nineteenth-century intellectual method. For it is only the lens of chronology that makes art appear to go forward. Respect for chronology would display Manet with Whistler, Monet, Renoir; but respect for visual affinities might display him with Hals, Velasquez, Goya.

I like to look at art in terms of the ever-shifting balance between schema and nature. For example, when Wordsworth was learning from the old English ballads, he was also studying from personal observation the language of contemporary farm laborers. The most beautiful and touching critical articulation of this typical dilemma of painting is to be found in Constable's letters. One minute he is praising Titian, Claude, Rubens, Ruysdael (what a mix is here! — Venetian, Roman, Flemish, Dutch); but on the next page Constable inveighs against the Academy for doing nothing else but study old art; he thinks painting will die of it. Nonetheless when he poses the model for the life class he sets her as Durer's Eve and is arrested on suspicion of stealing bushes which he is carrying to the Academy to create a Garden of Eden round her. But then he writes "When I sit down to make a sketch from nature, the first thing I do is to forget that I have ever seen a picture." But when he got his little studies indoors and began his large projects, the schema of Rubens's Chateau de Steen seems to have been thoroughly present to his mind's eye as a basis for his construction. This is apparent in a sketch version, at full size, for the large studio picture, *The Hay Wain*; while in its final finished version, the flickering light and breeze of the English weather is thrown like a coat over the Rubensian schema.

The unofficial artists of the 1960s were all variously involved in just this process: Porter, Katz and Freilicher took Abstract Expressionist, more particularly de Kooning's, brushwork and pitted it against direct observation, seeking the instantaneous glimpse, the surprise sensation; whatever labors their work may have cost them, theirs was an art that conceals art; it had the look of easy improvisation, as though the moving of paint collided accidentally with the description of an object. Welliver did something similar, with a nod to Homer and Elshemius for showing him a native American subject matter. Bell, Beck, and Resika worked with more evident schema from Italian and French painting, seeking in their paint handling and choice of motif the stability that comes from being aware of precedent.

They let their revisions stand on the canvas; for the more evident the schema the more it testifies to the artist's compositional as opposed to observational instinct, and the more thorough does the artist have to be to escape making souvenirs on the one hand, design on the other.

Like all artists they made rules for themselves; but they had an amusing way of turning a deaf ear to each other's dogma. Welliver once overheard Paul Georges advising some students to emulate the old rather than the modern masters, and summarized his advice as follows: "The upshot of it was he wanted more brown." When this remark was relayed to Rosemarie Beck she said, "Oh yes, I like brown very much." They tended to be somewhat reticent about subject matter — understandably, for as nothing was expected of them in this regard it was a tough problem to invent an iconography which would not acquire a momentum independent of the painting itself. Porter, who quoted Pasternak as saying "Poetry is in the grass," liked the almost accidental unpretentious domestic situations in Vuillard, the equivalent of which is available to any painter, and was pleased with the idea that poetry should be like the trollope Doll Tearsheet in *Henry IV*, "some road, as common as the way between St. Albans and London." When Resika was asked about his interest in landscape he quoted an interview with Jean Renoir:

> Critic: I notice there is a lot of nature in your films.
> Renoir: Thank you very much.

Nevertheless I believe that the upsurge of landscape painting did involve a critique and disavowal of the optimism of the technocrats which was to receive, by 1970, a death sentence from demographers and ecologists.

Compared with the great workshop and atelier traditions of the past and with the specialized aims of abstract artists the work of these painters would sometimes look ingenuous; but I found this vulnerability was part of their appeal, for vulnerability is a prerequisite of love (is this why Christians have to be exhorted to love God so often?); and do not all aesthetic judgments boil down in the end to statements of what you love?

III

My own relations with the work of these artists constituted my orientation as a painter starting out. I came to painting from a training in literary criticism, and my first efforts were more like theorems about paintings than actual paintings. I recall in art school being embarrassed by how to paint some tiny slivers of spandrels formed by a circle that was tangent to a square. Katz, my teacher, told me: "develop those forms." I bought some little sable brushes and poked about. Katz looked at it a week later and said — at a distance of 10 feet — "you faked it." I take that to have been my first lesson in painting as opposed to aesthetics. About this time I saw one painting each by Porter and Katz in an exhibition in the Yale Art Gallery (1961). Full of historicist expectations, I had no idea how to react. I dismissed it as rubbish. But Janet Fish said to me, "You're quite wrong. This is the latest thing that nobody can stand." I decided that these painters were Dadaists playing pranks at the expense of old-fashioned painting, and I continued trying to emulate Al Held's heroic geometries. But it seems to be a fate endemic to a modern painter to throw out his training and start from scratch. This happened to me through several simultaneous events. My work was obviously dependent on Held's and I felt cramped.

I also had the uncomfortable suspicion that I could not, even if I wanted to, paint a convincing representation of something. Then I met some young Greenbergers who asked me to exhibit with them. They published a statement, after agreeing not to, which asserted that art in the middle 1960s must be abstract, flat, and made of pure colors. I wished to disassociate myself from this silly bit of dogma. I had snakelike forms in my paintings and had been going to the zoo to draw snakes, so I added a head and a tail to one of these forms and hung the result in their show.

It was time to try what I feared I could not do. I decided that styles were a trap and that I would try to copy nature without one. I was in Maine. Maine farming has been deteriorating for 40 years, in consequence of which the unmown fields are grown up with bushes. I looked at these (one has no choice). They were the exact opposite of what I had been doing: they were round, not flat. They trembled in the breeze. They were made of myriads of constantly changing colors, and their edges merged imperceptibly into each other. It was immediately evident that there was no way to copy them, and the first question was what do you do with the paint? Abstract art has given us unforgettable lessons on that topic. The work of Katz and Porter were my guides, together with Katz's by now well-known statement "The paint moves across the surface making discriminations." My assumption was, the paint must flow, so I pushed it. These were discouraging days. I felt incompetent: why had I not learned to draw, and how do you match the colors out there? I read in an art magazine that Fairfield Porter had "opted out of the mainstream of modern art." That statement, which I now consider meaningless, made me feel bad. I found a cheap flat uptown; someone told me to move downtown so as not to be "left out."

In 1964 I saw the work of Joe Fiore at a Maine Coast Artists' show in Camden. I took him for a provincial buckeye painter; but I looked a second time, and the apparent *plainness* fascinated me: it approached the condition of stylelessness. I wanted to get rid of style, art, artiness, everything extra. I think this is what Stendhal meant when he said that every morning before writing on *The Charterhouse of Parma* he would read a few pages of the Civil Code. Fiore's art was especially appealing in the light of the official painting of the time, for Barnett Newman was then showing his *Stations of the Cross*, paintings which seemed to me to be scraping the barrel in terms of visual resources and creating a new high-water mark in terms of pretension and bombast.

If Joe Fiore read the Civil Code before going out on the motif it seemed to me that Paul Resika had been reading Pissarro's memoirs. His work looked both tender and well-educated as a result. He drew a distinction for me between the painters who push (which comes from Manet and Abstract Expressionism) and those who touch (which comes from Corot and Constable). His work made me feel naive and ignorant, but also wary: the day he looked at one of my pictures and said, "you need a man in a red cap, just — there!," the history of French painting from Corot onwards became for me an accelerating exercise in confectionery. Bonnard made me crave potatoes. I turned to the American primitives. I remember at the Whitney a painting of a man's farm with his cattle, family, and farm hands who were haying with scythes: a very big world in a very small compass. Its documentary quality was the antithesis of the insistent *art* component in modern art — the painter had not worn his sense of poetry on his sleeve. And my insurance company sent me Currier and Ives calendars; I like to think of those sincere narrators of rural life as my private equivalent of what farm laborers' diction was to Wordsworth — a plain way of saying it.

One day I watched Neil Welliver make a watercolor on his lawn. Instead of holding the brush nearly horizontal to the paper and spreading the wash, a technique modeled on Cotman that I had been taught in school in England, he held it nearly vertical and made long deliberate dashes and neat periods with it. I imitated this gesture in my studio (as I once had imitated that of Alex Katz who at the time had pushed his brush about in a sort of ragged star shape) and this evolved in my painting into an ornate surface which I intended to articulate like wrought iron.

Now it seemed to me that subject matter must *mean* something, otherwise why not paint abstractly? Welliver and Katz were both making a sort of mythology of the immediate and the personal, the particulars of their lives, their friends, their habitat, a touch of mock heroic humor in the one, a touch of urban irony in the other. About then I saw the last exhibition, before he died, of Charles Burchfield whose work combined the vision of the romantic poet with that of the naturalist. It is a vision that *reads* nature, for whom a wildflower is not a spot of color but a sign, revealing nature's processes. In it I recognized ways of looking at the country experience I loved in Maine. Rural life, the woods, the farms and panoramas, became my subject matter; I love disprized causes, and so did not avoid a spot, if it appealed to me, on the grounds that it was a conventional or hackneyed pretty view. Following Burchfield I tried to see the landscape as including legible stories as well as combinations of forms or qualities of light. In a first attempt at this idea I depicted, on the left of a painting, just milked cows resting in the shade at the back door of a barn. On the right the leader of the herd was already starting the procession towards a wagon of alfalfa that this farmer, short of pasture land, had provided for their feed. In the middle, others took a drink in the stream on their way. It was my first attempt to compose with live models. Oscar Wilde once remarked that "Cows are very fond of being photographed, and, unlike architecture, don't move."

I like to check my results with farmers who know their world, and I have a respect for topography, for I wish to find art in, not impose it on, the subject. But the slice of life is only part of an art; in a novel or a movie it takes its place in a larger composition; but in painting it needs reverberations that come from shaping to make it rich. So it was that I became interested in the work of Rosemarie Beck, who had become my favorite draftsman of all the painters. Her idealizing ambitions were a little strong for me at the time, and we quarreled: as when she declared that imagery didn't matter, it was the province of movie makers, and painting must concentrate on form. Or when she asserted, after seeing late Hals and the *Night Watch*, that good paintings are big, black, have many figures and are loosely painted, and that landscapes are not really paintings. Her massive rhythmic forms and the gouged-out alcoves of her amorous intellectual interiors seemed rich and powerful — rich in associations but powerfully present in themselves. She spoke of wholes against parts, of building and moving as opposed to putting and placing. Hers was an art of continual transition around forms, not across the surface. I realized that she was a brick builder and that I had been living in a world of figure skating. I remember thinking in about 1964 that a friend had trouble with the bottoms of his paintings. By 1968 these "bottoms" had become "foregrounds" for me.

By 1973 I thought of the foreground as an "entrance": for I felt that if you could not enter a painting you could not dwell in it, and if you could not dwell in it you could not dream in it. But I also saw in Leland Bell's work that you could build close to the surface too. Initially I had not responded to his work; I had been looking for lusher paint and something more innocently "lifelike." But the hammered-out decisions of his drawing, the rugged modeling and antiphony of hard colors and severe arabesques spoke to me of that antique thirst for the absolute in the actual.

Last year I visited Belgium and Holland. I expected to be interested in Dutch landscape but the Flemish primitives (who created such plentiful worlds and never kept you on the surface ensnared in their handling), and Breughel, interested me more. I quote from notes made in the Boymans van Beuningen Museum in Rotterdam: "Breughel's Toren von Babel reverses the scheme of the Impressionists and grand manner painters on whom I was reared. At one foot it is densely legible, a thousand stories in every square inch. At one hundred feet it is a magnificent abstraction. Photos of it are an absurdity. So *hard,* so right, at all distances as clear as crystal. *De loin* it makes the best Mondrian look flaccid and unresolved. Up close it is equivalent to two or three books of the Odyssey. The story continues into the deepest shadows — how lazy painters subsequently became. In every doorway (the largest is an inch and a half high) there are upwards of 20 figures, *all doing something, discriminated* in their activity. About 20 farms depicted in the middle distance. On the right an extensive ship-building industry, a merchant and fighting navy. A large boat propelled by oars, a building on fire, a distant island sparsely settled (5 or 6 buildings). On the left a river, 2 large ponds, woodchoppers, a man digging a well (or quarrying for rocks for the tower?), many thousands of cattle and sheep; some riverboats, horse-drawn carts at the foot of the tower, peculiar kiln constructions (or forts?), pumping systems for wells. On the tower various cranes, scaffolding, barrels; livestock continues to the third story. Forty-five boats *docked*, not counting boats moored or moving in the harbor. This picture made with one pinkish red, a yellowish white in the sky, green/blue clouds, a warm gray on the stones, Breughel brown in the foreground, an ocean blue (a little more cobalt than the left-hand landscape which is about the same as the clouds). Note the color of the building materials going up on the left." On the left of the tower are two colored vertical stripes, one pink, one gray-white. At the top of each are cranes. At the bottom of the pink one is a pile of bricks, at the bottom of the gray one a pile of stones. In St. Bavo's Cathedral in Ghent, home of the Van Eyck altarpiece, the columns and ribs of the vaults are gray stone, the faces of the vaults are pink brick.

In this painting it is Breughel's alert curiosity and relish for the whole observable world, in which the minute is the natural component, not enemy, of the grand; the fusing and playing against each other of the contemporary and the mythical, the literary, and the pictorial — in this comprehensive operation canons of aesthetics drop away and an epic appears on a modest canvas 30 inches by 24.

Breughel has an ethical message for us. His two intellectual friends were Fabiús of Bologna and Ortelius of Antwerp, the two great geographers of their day; geography was, at the time, the science that saw man as a part of a world much greater than himself. He never painted a town or urban complex, except this outrageous tower which I cannot help seeing as a symbol of hubris, of man too big for his boots. A modest sense of our place in relation to the whole is the lesson we, with our power to upset it, have yet to learn. When Breughel paints one of the ambitious adventures of man, like the fall of Icarus, he gives it a place, a very tiny place, in relation to the day-by-day preoccupations of people and the processes of nature. In 1915 Thomas Hardy wrote a fitting gloss:

> I
>
> Only a man harrowing clods
>   In a slow silent walk
> With an old horse that stumbles and nods
>   Half asleep as they stalk.
>
> II
>
> Only thin smoke without flame
>   From the heaps of couch grass;
> Yet this will go on the same
>   Though Dynasties pass.
>
> III
>
> Yonder a maid and her wight
>   Come whispering by;
> War's annals will fade into night
>   Ere their story die.

Originally delivered at Cedar Rapids Art Center, Iowa, in connection with the exhibition *A Sense of Place: The Artist and the American Land*, Nov. 29, 1973. First published in *Art Journal* XXXIV, Winter 1974/75. Reprinted here with the permission of the *Art Journal*.

WHAT REALISM MEANS TO ME (1981)

What is the appeal of realism in art? How does it work on us? What is it made of? What does it mean? When Shakespeare starts out a play with scenes in rhetorical blank verse announcing that the theme is the struggle for the English monarchy, why are we so pleased when he suddenly interrupts them with lines of slangy prose dialogue indicating that two teamsters are getting up before daylight, complaining what a terrible inn they're sleeping in — falling apart since Robin Ostler died, so bad they don't even provide a chamber pot, instead people use the fireplace full of last night's ashes, and this makes a lye where fleas breed, so this morning everyone's bitten all over: plus, someone tried to trick someone else out of their lantern, and the horses are stiff-jointed from the damp stables. What is the appeal of these scenes which, though they create a magically intense and precise atmosphere, do little to advance the action? In scenes like these Shakespeare's realism approaches comedy, but of a particular kind: an earthy contrast and counterpoint to the affairs of important people. We get sick of fine phrases and great causes, of aspirations and ambitions, of a nobility which may not be so noble — with their righteous civil wars (which may only be raw power grabs), their fussy sense of honor, their talk of peace and the national interest. And, whichever way we evaluate their motives and behavior, they are only part of the spectrum of life. That spectrum is what Shakespeare always has in mind. His realistic scenes put things in their place, sound notes that are essential to his totally inclusive, whole-society, 360° point of view. Breughel does this in his *Fall of Icarus*, where the event of the title is a tiny detail in a scene of ploughing and navigation. This painting, in which heroism seems positively esoteric in its relationship to daily life, is the opposite of Shakespeare's *Henry V*, where the enthusiasm of a military leader, his sense of national pride and purpose, can actually infect the most skeptical, recalcitrant, unmotivated, 'realistic' soldiers.

Perhaps there is an element of vanity in our liking for realism. Perhaps it is a question of wishing to see our own life in reflection, as a confirmation of our own existence and worth, as a verification of our own experiences. If it is, it's a situation that gives a boost to our self-confidence as art critics — we know all about *that* side of life: did the artist get it right? The vanity ingredient reaches an extreme development, so that it sometimes seems to split off from realism altogether, in the commission portrait — for instance, as practiced by Van Dyck and the English school that derived from him. Here the pleasure that comes from recognizing something we know has a twist to it — we are looking at an intentional, worked out, collaborative act by the patron-model and his knowing (but by no means necessarily insincere) accomplice, the artist. These two combine efforts to project an image, almost like advertising or propaganda, of wealth, rank, beauty, talent or whatever. But this kind of art is still not unlike realism in its appeal: that is to say, all of us have a showy streak, and can take pleasure in identifying with such an open, unfeigned indulgence of it; and so I find a touch of hypocrisy in the grumpy Marxist who objects to such paintings.

The realistic scenes in Shakespeare are scenes of lowlife, they have a class meaning to them, and this is a sense often given to the term "realism." It takes us outside the winnowed world of passions and ideals and confronts us with the functions of life, which are represented by the working class. But is this a necessary connection? Macbeth is a lord. By a series of drastic, monstrous moves he wins the crown of Scotland. At the end he is in a mood of frantic defiance as things turn against him. He begins a spiritual self-appraisal turning on the issue of how hardened he has become; he is interrupted with the news that Lady Macbeth is dead. "She should have died hereafter." That is his reaction. The psychology is intensely realistic. Macbeth's circuits are completely overloaded, the most he can do with bad news is to deflect it. This is not consoling realism, a realism that confirms our sense of what life is like; it extends it, it makes us stop and think. It can be shocking, and has nothing to do with class. Where comic low-life scenes present the rounded-out spectrum of life and extend our sense of what things are by relating them to one another, so those moments (equally typical of Shakespeare) that are psychologically penetrating, like certain portraits or paintings of dramatic incidents by Rembrandt or Titian, deepen our sense of the complications inside a human head.

But Shakespeare, or Titian for that matter, inherited a sense of order from the Middle Ages in which everything in the universe was arranged in a tidy system from God through the angels down to man, then animals, trees, stones and so forth. It was an interconnected hierarchy in which everything had a fixed place. Such was the background to the discovery of America. Whereas nowadays, in relation to the background we've inherited, when you read on the front page of the newspaper about the discovery of another "black hole," it is, quantitatively and qualitatively, a bit like finding a pinhole caused by rust on the bottom of your colander. Today to find a sense of completeness in their lives, an overall coherence, people move to the country, build homemade houses out of reach of the electric grid, raise their own food, start their own schools. And the kind of counterpoint we get in art today is not between the low-life and the heroic scenes, the tragic and the comic, all in the same play. The range of experience today is articulated by the distance between different artists. If Agnes Martin is the ascetic St. Simon Stylites of contemporary painting, Richard Bosman might be considered its Sancho Panza or its Caliban. Are they perhaps the related parts of some great embracing structure like a gothic cathedral, which encompasses the delicate and noble traceries of a rose window as well as the grotesque fantasy of some weird gargoyle? Or are they the jarring, mutually uncomprehending voices of a Tower of Babel? And what would be the position of the realist in all this?

The way realism works makes me think of something someone once told me about the Michelin guides. The French tire company puts out two sets of guides to the countries of Europe; the red one tells you about the hotels and restaurants, the green one advises you on how to go about experiencing the cultural and historical aspects of the country. They put out a green guide to New York City. As one of the three star attractions they recommend, so I was told, that visitors station themselves outside the Wall Street subway station at about 4:45 p.m. to watch the spectacle of 'le rush hour'. It seems to me that the Michelin guide-writers would do quite a good job of training young realists, for this is one of the things that realists do: they look at the common, everyday aspects of life with the fresh, surprised interest and curiosity of the traveler in a foreign country. What may very well be a boring, tiring, uncomfortable, humiliating daily routine to a brokerage clerk is a marvelous sight to a French tourist. In the 1960s middle-class suburbanites organized bus tours of New York City's East Village to look at the hippies and their *modus vivendi*.

Abbie Hoffman, I think it was, organized a reverse of this tour, and took a busload of hippies on a sightseeing visit to suburban middle-class Queens. Through the metaphor of travel everything comes alive. Except that the traveler's picture is half a picture: he is euphoric on exotica and the novelty of it all. This may be O.K. for a romantic; but the realist needs to know his subject like a resident too. The traveler sees that farmland is pretty; this doesn't concern the farmer at all, even if he had time to notice it. He's preoccupied with the fact that his topsoil is poor or his heifers got out. It's a common rift in experience; what we're outside of we don't really understand, what we're inside of we can't really see. The farmer is like the poet Su Shih who in 1084 wrote this on the wall at West Forest Temple:

> From the side, a whole range; from the end,
>   a single peak:
> Far, near, high, low, no two parts alike.
> Why can't I tell the true shape of Lu-Shan?
> Because I myself am in the mountain.

One of my favorite travelers is William Cobbett, an English farmer's son born in 1762, who happened on a copy of Swift's *Tale of a Tub* while young, ran away from home, joined the army, was shocked by the corruption he ran into there, and emerged a political reformer. He was court-martialled, exiled from England, spent time in America pamphleteering against republicanism under the name of Peter Porcupine (he was subjected to counter-attacks by a certain Paul Hedgehog) and studying the agriculture on Long Island, some features of which he imported back to England. At home again he made a series of tours of the English Countryside on horseback in order to study the real state of agriculture and the condition of the farmworkers. His reports appeared in the form of a journal in the *Political Register,* a magazine he edited himself; later he made them into a book titled *Rural Rides*. Cobbett sees the countryside as a habitat for humans; he writes about it from the point of view of its authentic inhabitants, those who have the most stake in it — the people who make their living from the land. He does not sentimentalize rural life, he does not ask nature to supply his spiritual needs, nor does he use it as a dictionary of novel shapes, colors and anecdotes. He sees its relationship to the city, its part in the whole society. Because of his farming origins and political experience he is the traveler and the resident at once. It was the beginning of the Industrial Revolution, there was a tremendous social upheaval going on, things were in atrocious condition. But unlike some Depression photographers who seem rhapsodic over tattered clothes, tumble-down shacks and weather-beaten skin, Cobbett only gets enthusiastic when he finds a fine, early field of turnips, improved prices at market, villagers resourcefully frugal and neatly dressed. Charity passed out with religious education, an activity sponsored by aristocrats, he regards as a cause of hypocrisy. When conditions look bad he turns around and attacks 'the THING', by which he means the political and economic system comprising outrageous policies, greedy middlemen, specious intellectuals, indolent landowning Lords, and the city of London itself which he called "the insatiable Wen." He calculates that farm laborers produce fifteen times as much food as they receive under the current wage system, and that this wealth is sucked up by this "wen" on the landscape.

Here is E.M. Forster, another traveler I love, with very different preoccupations than Cobbett, including in a fictional incident in his novel *A Passage to India* an awareness of just the complications I'm talking about:

> "They wandered over the old fort, now deserted, and admired the various views. The scenery, according to their standards, was delightful — the sky grey and black, bellyfuls of rain all over it, the earth pocked with pools of water and slimy with mud. A magnificent monsoon — the best for three years, the tanks already full, bumper crops possible."

Maybe these are not the most beautiful sentences Forster wrote — he was more at home with human nature than with agriculture and irrigation; but they show him to be alert to what a lot may be going on in the seemingly innocent act of looking at a view. An artist's openness to the rich, endless complexities of that situation, the nuances involved in it and the numerous ways of playing with it, makes it possible for something to become a revelation when it might so easily have been a boring iteration of facts.

The borderline between the two is exceedingly interesting to me, and some artists I admire a lot liked to sail very close to the wind on this issue. Chekhov, playwright, storywriter, doctor, spent nine months of his short life journeying six thousand miles across Russia under circumstances that were sometimes quite dangerous (there was no trans-Siberian railway yet) to write a report on the penal colony on the island of Sakhalin that lies off the coast of Russia just north of Japan. He made this journey on his own initiative and believed firmly in the importance of his report. Among other things he apparently made a census, single-handed, of the population of the entire colony. Constable, who once declared that painting was a branch of natural philosophy — that is to say, science — is known for the meteorological accuracy of his skies. His brother was a miller, and he is on record as having said, "When I look at a mill painted by John, I see that it will *go round*, which is not always the case with those by other artists." Here is Constable, in a lecture on the art of landscape painting, discussing a picture by the seventeenth-century Dutch painter Ruysdael:

> "*We see nothing truly till we understand it*...This picture represents an approaching thaw. The ground is covered with snow, and the trees are still white; but there are two windmills near the center; the one has the sails furled, and is turned in the position from which the wind blew when the mill left off work, the other has the canvas on the poles and is turned another way, which indicates a change in the winds; the clouds are opening in that direction, which appears by the glow in the sky to be the south (the sun's winter habitation in our hemisphere), and this change will produce a thaw before the morning. The occurrence of these circumstances show that Ruysdael *understood* what he was painting."

Saenredam, who painted church interiors in seventeenth-century Holland, was originally an antiquarian who set out to make drawn records of the churches and civic buildings of Amsterdam, Haarlem and Utrecht. Before he made a painting from one of these drawings he worked out construction drawings of ground plans and elevations, made with instruments and based on the measurements of the buildings. His painting of the Old Town Hall of Amsterdam he made from such drawings some five years after the building had been torn down and replaced by a new hall, and fifteen years after he had made the drawings. The City of Amsterdam bought his painting as a record of its past. Saenredam's passion for facts, his desire for exactitude, the intense self-restraint necessary in his kind of work, makes for a sort of urgent dryness, an excruciatingly low-keyed, almost insensible skin-of-the-teeth element of poetry in his painting, sharp vinegar to what Kenneth Koch called 'any "kiss-me-I'm-poetical" junk': a kind of poetry that is all the more intriguing because seemingly unconcerned about its own existence.

Restraint is often one of the qualities of realism. When artists shift their attention from their own reactions to observation of the object, the reactions have no release; if there is a temperament there, it gets worked into the statement of the facts, where it doesn't draw attention to itself. I find this restraint in the sober portraits of the sixteenth-century painter Moroni. It's often in Constable too, in his paintings of the unspectacular East Anglia countryside; sometimes it comes out as a sort of affectionate patience with the desultory pace of provincial life. And it's sometimes in Theodore Rousseau too, especially when he compresses his often quite wild talent onto a very small canvas.

William Blake wrote a poem I cannot help connecting with this subject:

> Never seek to tell thy love,
> Love that never told can be;
> For the gentle wind does move
> Silently, invisibly.
>
> I told my love, I told my love,
> I told her all my heart;
> Trembling, cold, in ghastly fears,
> Ah! she doth depart.
>
> Soon as she was gone from me,
> A traveler came by,
> Silently, invisibly:
> He took her with a sigh.

I think of this poem as being in one sense a comment on the deceptively polite novels of E.M. Forster, where extraordinary revelations happen to people — silently, invisibly — in a wood, or a cave, or an archeological site.

Sometimes there is a note of self-depreciation mixed in with the qualities I'm talking about, as when James Schuyler writes that his aim in poetry is "merely to say, to see and say, things / as they are." (I'm focusing on that "merely.") But this self-depreciation is probably not to be taken at face value. E.M. Forster uses the idea in *Howards End*. This novel, which Lionel Trilling described as being "about England's fate," has for a first sentence, "One may as well begin with Helen's letters to her sister." It's a way of cutting out the pompous, the pretentious, the grandiose, the overweight. In Forster it may be a reaction to the puffed-out-chest openings of heavy Victorian novels. It's a method, in other words, of intellectual accuracy, of emotional accuracy; it says, "A little deflation, if you don't mind please, in the interest of *no false sentiments*." Chekhov takes a slightly different approach to a similar end: he warns another author who is writing a story about a wounded elk, "The piece has to be written in the style of a police report.... Should you moisten the language with a tear you will deprive the subject of its sternness and of everything deserving attention." And Stendahl claims that when he was working on *The Charterhouse of Parma* he would read a few pages of the Civil Code every day before sitting down to write.

There is a particular group of Chekhov stories that are of intense interest to me. They are the rather long ones he wrote towards the end of his life; in them there are really no heroes or heroines but groups of more or less equally important main characters; there is usually no central event, but a chain of them: and no point is being made. One of them is called *Three Years*, a title that fascinates for its refusal to highlight or single anything out. Another is called *The Murder*. It concerns a fundamentalist, a zealot, who has left the church which he now reviles, and celebrates Mass himself at home. Home is a roadside tavern he keeps, a squalid place where he lives with his wife and daughter. His cousin, who has quit working and is unable to provide for himself on account of some vague illness, considers the innkeeper a heretic and reproaches him continually. The place is overcrowded; its inhabitants are irritable; there is some suspicion the out of work cousin may have money stashed away. The family entanglements, the financial problems, the religious conflict, the squalor, the weather, the minds of the protagonists which are unable to grasp or explain to themselves what is going on — Chekhov makes no comment on these details; through them he states the case. When the actual murder happens it is hardly more emphasized than a horse stuck in the snow, or the inconvenience of a mislaid waterbucket; and no one seems to be decisively more right or wrong than anyone else. Chekhov doesn't say, don't mess with fundamentalists or, don't have your cousins to stay or, we need better housing conditions in Russia. The events one has just read about are horrible: but mainly one feels the acuteness of Chekhov's perceptions. His artistry says, to judge is presumptuous, to generalize is glib. What counts is to observe intensely, and when you do so you feel not so much inclined to advocate your opinion.

Chekhov got into trouble for writing like this. Soon after he started publishing stories in magazines it appears that his editors, Suvorin of *New Times* and Plesheyev of the *Northern Herald*, both separately wrote to him saying they liked his stories, they wanted his stories, but whose side was he on? Was he a liberal, a conservative, for the regime, against the church? He replied, it is my job to state the question correctly.

In life, the quality of being observant is something we enjoy, something we respect — "Oh, so you noticed!" It indicates a connection made, the possibility of empathy, the traveler identifying with the resident. And, while all of us are ready enough with an opinion, we are not often really interested in finding out the whole story. As the historian Gibbon said, "It is opinion, not truth, that travels the world without a passport." So realism, in elevating the art of being intensely, thoroughly observant, expresses a set of values. It is a long way from the neutral, impotent, soulless transcription of life that it is sometimes taken to be — even by Chekhov himself who, in one of those moments of rather tough self-evaluation that artists seem to go through, declared himself disappointed with his own work and with that of his whole generation: "We have neither immediate nor distant aims, and our souls are a yawning void. We have no politics, we don't believe in revolution, we have no God, we are not afraid of ghosts, and I personally am not afraid even of death and blindness. One who desires nothing, hopes for nothing, and fears nothing cannot be an artist."

I like Chekhov much better than he did the day he wrote that. And I would contrast his artistic method with, for one, that of Dickens — George Orwell spoke of "Dickens' habit of telling small lies in order to emphasize what he regards as a big truth" — and with Maupassant for another. Maupassant is also called a realist. But the Maupassant method is to sieve, ferociously, till he has isolated one extremely compact, clear-cut action, often exemplifying an abstract quality which in turn sometimes serves for the story's title — "Imprudence," or "Regret." In "Regret" an aging bachelor wakes up one dismal autumn morning feeling extremely dissatisfied with his life. He remembers his youthful passion for the wife of his next door neighbor, and how the three of them had once gone on a picnic together; while the husband was sleeping off his lunch, he and the wife had sauntered off into the woods...and then returned to the sleeping husband. So, on this bleak morning many years later he runs across the street, bursts in on his neighbor who is now a widow, and reminds her of the incident. Oh yes, she remembers. "And is it possible," he says, "if I had been more enterprising...?" "Of course, you booby." He is ushered out by the maid. Now while this story is brilliant and witty, it is also a little mean-spirited; it is a wickedly partial vignette cut out from the complexity and continuity of life. What we like about it is the little point it makes. Things are not observed as interesting in themselves, but as though they were type-cast character actors co-opted to serve the story's plan. Sentences follow one another like runners in a relay team, their eye on the finish-line. The story is a set-up, like a *conte moral*. But instead of holding up an example of good conduct, Maupassant is a moral muckraker, and his "realism" (if that is what it is) proceeds from an attitude which says with a grin, "Your fragrant drawing rooms are all a sham. Just let me open that closet door and show you all the skeletons in there." Where Maupassant picks things out with a spotlight from one acute angle, Chekhov shines floods from all around; he shows events in their context like gold in the matrix. Differentiation between foreground and background disappears, and the real hero turns out to be the texture of life. The realization that events have happened sneaks up on one like those realizations in our own lives that children grow up and adults grow old.

Parallels to this contrast of methods suggest themselves in terms of painting; for instance, in the way Rubens shows you around his newly-acquired country place the Chateau de Steen with exhilarated rapidity and an eye for the typical, rushing you off into the distance like the pilot of a tiny plane skimming the hedges in an eager take-off; while Constable, who borrowed a lot from Rubens's compositions, wanders through the landscape of *The Hay Wain* at a more ruminative pace, allowing himself to be diverted by a gentle, affectionate attention to the individual things around him.

So far I have been talking about something I've called "realism" as though it was an attitude to life, and as though it belonged to no particular time, place or even specific art form. But realism in painting today seems to me to have sprung from an attitude to painting more than an attitude to life. For instance, I first became involved with realism when I felt stuck as an abstract painter — stuck with a set of moves I was repeating. When I started to paint directly from nature it was in order to place a trip-wire or obstacle in front of me to upset that set of moves; in order to get that over there down on canvas, I said to myself, you'll have to take a whole new look at your paints and your procedures. So instead of being a way of using painting to look at nature, it was a way of using nature to force on yourself fresh ways of looking at painting. This seems to be what Impressionism meant to Fairfield Porter; he wrote:

> "In their passivity before nature, and in having to learn everything by themselves, they came upon new qualities in pigment. They portrayed no ideas from outside of painting in their preoccupation with painting as a

WHAT REALISM MEANS TO ME

working of material. What does the paint look like, what does it do?"

One of the side effects of modernism and abstract art was to upset and clear away old painting methods, training systems, traditions, so you could start representing again as though from zero. This was certainly what made the already exhibiting artists I was very interested in when I started painting from nature — Fairfield Porter, Alex Katz, Neil Welliver, Joe Fiore, to name a few — exciting. They were not involved with the practice of an old craft, but with making discoveries. They made you feel that the question of what the world looked like was a wide open one. So personally when I hear realists today berate and beleaguer modernism, I'm inclined to think they might with as much justice bring a paternity suit against it instead.

For me things went something like this: you mix up some yellow paint and put it down in a certain context and it turns into a patch of sunlight on green grass. Fascinated, you try it again, each time getting more particular about the color and the shape. You concentrate very intently on what you are looking at, you stop making paintings in the studio from sketches and work exclusively from nature because you want to be responding to something actual, not yet translated into flat shapes and definite colors, over every millimeter of the canvas. An interest in facts, in Constable's meteorology, in topographical engravings or documentary photographs, comes about as a way of putting something else ahead of aesthetic decisions; not, Shall this composition be symmetrical or asymmetrical but, What shapes and colors will result if I ask the painting to describe this? Not, Is this beautiful? but, Did I get it all in? Painting from nature might be thought of as a way of consciously setting things up so you could paint unselfconsciously. This is a quality I like in naive art. Apollinaire quotes a critic who wrote about le douanier Rousseau as saying, "Now the majority of the works one sees at the Independents suffer precisely from this defect: their creators *thought about them*. Only the gentle Douanier Rousseau would have been incapable of *wanting* to do what he did." I believe this is because of the method of naive painters who, being unschooled, are unaware of the metaphorical conventions of the language of painting and do not cultivate a mastery of them. They try to mainline straight to the subject as best they can. A lot of naive paintings for instance look like inventories of things. However wild their style may look to a sophisticated viewer, its motive was literalist. When Rousseau painted a portrait of Apollinaire, to ensure a good likeness he measured his face.

There is one thing I think realism is definitely not, though it is often confused with it, and that is a technique. Technique is a skill you can learn so you don't have to respond to what you are looking at, you don't have to be inquisitive about it. If something is real to you, the question becomes, not How do I do that, but Wha*t* is this phenomenon I'm perceiving? When a painter is armed with technique, technique is what you see in the painting, technique is what is real in it. Nineteenth-century French and English academy painting, with its minute details, expresses the attitude "I know what the world looks like, and I have the expertise to portray it." It resembles the work of the Russian social realist painter Fairfield Porter described: "The artist knows everything and uses his eyes only to keep his hand from slipping." The Flemish primitives like Van der Goes say with amazement, "so that's what the world looks like!" and this amazement is reflected in the freshness and affection with which each detail is recorded on their oak panels.

I doubt if anyone today can set about making realism in the spirit that, perhaps, the Florentines thought about it in 1450. The idea that you might really be able to imitate reality, and prove you had done so because you could know exactly what reality is by measuring it, as in perspective, or cutting it up, as in anatomy, seems too simple today. The fact is that one way we look at landscapes is so to speak episodically, the way a butterfly gathers pollen, leaping from one center of interest to another. So the experience of looking at a Chinese mountainscape with its misty lacunae, is as real (maybe more so) as looking at a painstaking documentation of every intervening inch. Consciousness itself is as real as what is out there, and can in fact be isolated from what is out there, as it is possible to make a novel or a poem out of the meditations of a nameless, disembodied voice. Also, painting has been deprived of many of its old objective functions. Suppose today a painter wanted to do Saenredam all over again from nature. We have other ways to make records of our buildings. So it would not be a matter of putting art into making the record of a building, but of putting the record of a building into making art. What with Saenredam was the occasion or pretext for art is now an art idea in itself.

So today one chooses to work as a "realist" consciously, aware of these things, and I think it would require a certain stiffness of mind, an insistence — which some artists do indeed have, and are proud of it, and put it bluntly in their painting — to ignore all that and say, "This way really is realistic." I don't think it's so simple. I rather think you choose to take, among many possible ones, this particular route to the real. Because you don't wave yourself or your methods under the nose of the viewer, maybe you should describe yourself as a poker-faced painter. That is to say, the realist, during a day's work, may feel a huge wave of sentimental affection for his motif, or see in it a set of geometrical relationships that would make it look as angular as Mondrian's ocean. These experiences are real; they may even have a discreet life somewhere in a realist painting. But they are not what is presented first. On the way to style there are denials as well as affirmations.

Sometimes I think about Fats Waller. When we listen to some old crooner gushing away we bring our own sense of irony to the experience and call it "camp." But Fats Waller takes a different way with the same shop-worn song. He doesn't trash the sentimental tunes he jokes around with; on the contrary, he gives them back to us. As Shakespeare keeps the scathing Mercutio around while Romeo meets Juliet, so Waller includes in his restatement of those tunes a good-natured, "realistic" recognition of the fact that, yes they sure are overblown, and once you've admitted that, you can enjoy them again and even accept their now deflated sentiments. So it may very well be that for some realists today a certain self-consciousness, even tinged with mischief, has been duly emulsified with the sincerity. So their work would not insist "This is what is really real," but say instead "I'm going to see just how absolutely dead straight I can be about this."

Today among the realists one finds a huge diversity of approaches, but just about all of them contain elements of naturalism. Three kinds of naturalism interest me; the naturalism of the part, the naturalism of the whole and "helpless" naturalism. By naturalism of the part I mean the way Van Eyck in the Annunciation scene on the Ghent altarpiece shows you the Virgin in every detail, the hair, clothes, jewelry and so on, as well as her room and everything in it including a view out the window on to the real town of Ghent. But the Virgin is much too big to stand up in her own room. Clearly the room is compressed to include as many details of it as possible, and the Virgin enlarged for the same reason — if in fact Van Eyck had thought about their relationship in "realistic" terms at all. Early Flemish painters learned a lot about painting figures from sculpture, where the figures have no "background." So the landscapes or rooms in these paintings are less the world or space that figures inhabit than additional contrasting worlds, with their own separate spaces. The Pissarro of the Rouen Market, from the Metropolitan Museum, is an example of the naturalism of the whole. Here it is how things fit together and amalgamate that comes first: to display the total bustle of the marketplace at the foot of a towering cathedral. Details of the individual people are sacrificed for this. By 'helpless' naturalism I mean the naturalism of the naive painters I have already mentioned; for instance that of John Kane, the Scotch-Irish day laborer who painted views of Pittsburgh, the town where he spent much of his working life. Here the possibility of representation clearly seems magical to the artist, and at the same time he is so handicapped by lack of training and knowledge that one feels his immense struggle and complete vulnerability in trying to bridge this gap; as well as the complete sincerity of his feeling for the town where he made his home and from which, by working in its freight yards and on its construction sites, he derived a sense of pride and meaning for his life. With a heartbreaking mixture of crudeness and subtlety, Kane puts this town before you. His experience with the art of painting is like the second of the two described in this stanza of one of George Herbert's poems:

> A man that looks on glass
> On it may stay his eye;
> Or if he pleaseth, through it pass,
> And then the Heaven espy.

Originally delivered at the symposium *Contemporary American Realism Since 1960* at the Pennsylvania Academy of the Fine Arts, October 17, 1981. First published in a PAFA publication of the proceedings, 1982. Reprinted here with permission of the Pennsylvania Academy of the Fine Arts.

THE TENSES OF LANDSCAPE (1996)

> *The earth, in fact, was a stretch of time.*
>
> — Laura Riding

I was born and raised in England and I think this has something to do with my attitude toward landscape. I don't have what I perceive as a New World sense of an antithesis between unspoiled nature and human culture; a landscape to me is a place where people live and work. There really was no wild nature in the South of England where I grew up and in Europe, as George Orwell said, "Every step you take you're probably treading on ten dead people." Already by the first century C.E., a great proportion of Europe was penetrated by Roman roads. Whereas local roads tended to follow irregular courses that yielded to the physical characteristics of the terrain, the Romans preferred to build their roads in straight lines expressing a will to dominate and manipulate the landscape for human convenience and control. This will was expressed in other things the Romans did. The eroded hillsides of Calabria and Basilicata which to this day support only a rather feeble growth of stunted trees, are the result of the drastic clear-cutting the Romans practiced in order to heat their immense bath houses.

The Campagna around Rome itself once consisted of stable small farms worked by peasants practicing a sustainable agriculture, i.e. raising a variety of crops and livestock. When the inhabitants left these farms in large numbers to fill the huge military drafts that took place during the Punic Wars, the countryside was taken over by land barons who practiced intensive monoculture, often with prisoner-of-war labor. The soil was quickly exhausted by this type of farming; the land was consequently abandoned, and turned into malarial swamp. It still has — at least when I was last there — the feeling of a ghostly wasteland dotted with masonry, the scabs of antiquity hanging on.

We commonly sense a difference between various kinds of human intervention in the landscape though, and in fact, the cultures that built the megaliths at Stonehenge or Carnac, or cut the huge white men and horses into the chalk hills of southern England, do not seem to us exploitative or destructive in their physical impact on the landscape compared with the Romans. Nonetheless, our culture generally applauds Roman engineering, along with the engineering of our own time, as achievements in the name of progress, a word beloved by the proponents of the Industrial Revolution, who considered that their inventions would improve the lot of mankind, making us all more comfortable and happier. They thought of their tremendous engineering feats as the first of their kind since the ancient cultures of Egypt, Babylon, Rome, and they applied a historicizing architectural ornamentation to these modern constructions that was meant to evoke that comparison. But with each step forward in the name of progress we seem to feel that there has been an attendant loss, and it often seems to be the role of landscape imagery to express or assuage this feeling. It is a role assumed by some of the great masters of European landscape painting. In contrast to Dutch seventeenth-century landscape painters, who tend to express great optimism about the expanding agriculture and manufacturing of a newly independent state, Constable, stylistically innovative, is deeply retrospective in his landscape sensibility at a time of drastic changes and social unrest in the English countryside. Also, things that must have once seemed like interpolations in the landscape become, to later generations, the very thing they feel they are losing, have lost, or wish they had. Claude Lorraine used the triumphs of Roman engineering to help him image a timeless world where man's ambition seems both magnificent and reconciled with nature; while in Corot's work, Roman ruins have become organic parts of the landscape. Here we are dealing with a question of assimilation that is both mental (we get used to things) and physical (they decay).

The issue of loss seems a particularly sensitive one in the North American situation, because when the Europeans came here they found nature in a peculiarly abundant and pristine state compared with what they had left behind. The accounts by early explorers of the flora and fauna they found are almost ecstatic. In the nineteenth century the French etcher, Rodolphe Bresdin, made a pilgrimage here to find what he thought he could find nowhere else, virgin forests. Even today some bits of these survive. But I don't think "virgin nature" is an adequate description of what the Europeans found. I think they found human societies that were not interested in a progressive notion of culture but in a cyclical idea of life. Even what Europeans have taken to be one of the most (in our own terms) "advanced" forms of New World culture, the Mayan calendar, is a cyclical account of time. Nature in these cyclical societies is not something for people to overcome because it is not something separate: people are part of it. At the first Earth Day in 1970, I remember a Native American speaker saying, "If the white man does not respect his mother the earth and his father the sun, he will not endure." This did not sound gratuitous, it did not sound like hyperbole. But even though our progressive society has come to acknowledge the truths that are expressed by cyclical societies, I don't see any vigorous attempts to incorporate these truths into our physical lives. Our biologists deplore the loss of biodiversity, but progressive societies have almost completely eradicated any surviving cyclical ones whose mode of existence fosters that diversity. Our present fascination with virtual reality and information networks demonstrate that we really don't believe E.M. Forster's forebodings about the dystopian technological nightmare depicted in his novella *The Machine Stops*, where physical reality has been almost abolished and all that remains is comfort and ideas. That nightmare is our new playground. One of the few movements that seriously and effectively backs off from our progressive culture is the organic gardening and farming movement, which began to grow and take on significance in response to the sort of revelations about what is happening to the environment contained in Rachel Carson's *Silent Spring*. To me the interest of this movement is less in its effort to put food on the market that is healthier for humans, than in its intent to take plentiful crops off the land and at the same time leave that land in better condition than the farmer found it; to use no substances in this process that would be toxic to any life in the environment, and to create no waste products that cannot be absorbed back into the farming process. This is not an agriculture that expresses a desire to return to something lost, it is a hopeful agriculture that expresses faith in the future.

So I would concur with the philosopher Edmund Leites in seeing a lot of ambivalence in the overall picture of our attitude to the relationship between progress and nature. We may yearn for a past, real or fictional, but we go forward anyway. Here is a contradiction involving time. We create nature reservations, while living somewhere where nature is largely excluded or, as we think, under control. Here is a contradiction involving space. In another spatial contradiction we try to hide the price of progress from ourselves, to turn our backs on it, a point made by Ann Bermingham in her book *Landscape and Ideology* where she tells of a development in the early years of the Industrial Revolution: while the factory owners of the late eighteenth century like Josiah Wedgwood lived at their factories, later owners, as the factories got grimmer, moved away, lived elsewhere. This trend continues in our own time, where we take the profits from a polluted industrial park and spend them buying a cottage by an unspoiled stream. When I choose images for my paintings, I'm especially attracted to sites which bring together separated realities like these, realities which are really functions of one another, and which we need to connect again in order to see holistically what we are doing. For instance, the painting *U.S. Scrap Metal Gets Shipped For Reprocessing in Southeast Asia, Jersey City,* 1994, represents a cove on New York Harbor, just south of the Statue of Liberty. To the left of centre is a new condominium development built on an old pier, and expressing both by its architecture (a sort of sheetrock-Chateau style) and its name (Port Liberté) a certain social pretension. The condo residents like living here because there's a direct ferry to the financial district of New York, where many of them work (you can see the World Trade Centre on the far left of the painting), and where electronic transactions of an extraordinary degree of abstraction take place. An example of the concrete physical results of such transactions is happening right across the cove from the condo (on the right hand side of the painting) where scrap metal is being sorted, baled and loaded into barges which are then pulled out to deep water and reloaded onto ocean-going ships which carry it to Southeast Asia; there it will be made into Hondas and transistors, and shipped back to us. In the middle of the cove is a sign of the decay of industrial life, rotting supports for a pier that once carried an oil pipeline connecting tankers in the deep water to the refineries on shore. Around the cove marsh grasses flourish in the interstitial areas we haven't yet found a use for. Canada geese congregate on warm sandy banks exposed by the low tide, and egrets feed in the shallows in front of the barges.

In The High Island Oil Field, February, After the Passage of a Cold Front, 1990, depicts an oil field, long past its prime, on the Texas coast. It represented for me an accommodation, a sort of peaceable kingdom. The pumps are on raised platforms because this land, which is at sea level, floods during a hurricane. Cows, horses and wading birds share this 1200 acre field with the pumps, and when strong winds blow in from the north after the passage of a cold front, the sediments that are pumped up with the oil and natural gas and which collect in the bottoms of ditches, are stirred up so the ditch water looks red. The perspective down the centre of this painting is the raised embankment of an old railroad bed. The cows like to congregate and lie down to rest on this long-infertile ground because it dries off quickly after a rain; and so they dung it up intensively too. So, it is gradually beginning to regain fertility and support a sparse cover of weeds which spread in by runners from either side of the embankment. Here the tenses of a landscape imagery which represents what is lost or threatened are reversed; we see decaying industrialization being replaced or reclaimed by the progress of nature. These weeds interest me more than ancient redwoods; they are the vanguard of nature's forces as she wages *her* war back on us; or perhaps I should say, here nature reembraces us, her prodigal sons and daughters. These weeds give the idea of nature not as a state we've lost but as a process with a future.

My paintings are executed from start to finish on site in the landscape and take months. When you work outdoors, you surrender a lot of control over your subject and that is what I like about it, the interactive, experiential character of it. It is the opposite of starting with a clear-cut idea and projecting that into the work. You learn about the site as you proceed; no matter what thoughts or opinions I may have about what is there when I begin, what comes to concern me as I work are the things themselves, not any sense I make of them. I made an oil sketch one April in response to the huge scale of a scrap metal pile towering over the fence in front of it. When I returned to the site with a large canvas made to proportions that would give me room for those two leading players, the pile was gone, sold to the Japanese. Did that mean I no longer had a subject? Well, no: it meant I followed what was *now* actually offered at the site. (*A Fence at the Periphery of a Jersey City Scrap-Metal Yard,* 1993). The ground, bare in spring, produced a fine crop of weeds as summer wore on, and the fence became a subject in itself; perforated by tiny holes that let the wind through, it allowed you to sense mysteriously the semi-visible operations going on inside it. So, working from nature is not a technical issue; it has to do with letting the realities of the outside world impinge on and steer the activities of your own artistic world.

I've talked a lot about "imagery." This term, like its sibling "narrative," are almost unavoidable in aesthetic discussions today. That's o.k. provided we recognize them for what they are: x-ray terms. They look through or past the art-work's body. But in art it is often the body more than the imagery that really signifies. In his essay about Swift's *Gulliver's Travels* called "Politics vs. Literature," George Orwell deals with the role of "imagery" or "narrative" in works of art, and the question of our endorsing, or not, the point of view expressed by them. He says *Gulliver's Travels* has always been one of his favorite books, he's read it 8 or 10 times, and he believes his taste in this is not aberrant because the book has never been out of print since its first publication and has been translated into some 20 languages. But, he says, the point of view of this book, its attitude to life, could not be more antithetical to his own. He hates its know-nothing attitude to science and knowledge, its disgust with the human body, its belief in an over-organized state based on a kind of slave population. So how can he love it? In his answer he does not praise its formal beauties; he says, rather, that the point of view it represents is something that is a component, even though only a small or partial one, of what we all feel, sometimes. There are days when any of us might wake up having thoughts like that about life. I would extrapolate from this and say that nothing could be more disappointing to me than to go to a show and find that it contained nothing but works expressing a point of view about landscape similar to my own; and that art moves us when the point of view, no matter what that is — (provided, as Orwell says, it is not insane) — is strongly, finely, richly, subtly, poignantly or in whatever way, embodied in the piece.

Is there really an opposition between nature and progress? For me, the answer is partly real, partly linguistic. I find I use the word nature in two ways. One is as used by Schiller in his essay *Naive and Sentimental Poetry*, 1795, who speaks of nature as meaning "plants, minerals, animals and landscapes, as well as human nature in children, in the customs of country folk, and the primitive world." "Nature, considered in this wise, is for us nothing but the voluntary presence, the subsistence of things on their own, their existence in accordance with their own immutable laws." I take "voluntary" to mean "not through the agency of humans." Then there is the sense used by Buckminster Fuller, quoted by the poet Gary Lenhart as saying "If it isn't nature it doesn't exist." Here nature means everything that exists physically, since everything is subject to the laws of nature, including man's inventions.

Since the practice of the simplest forms of agriculture, e.g. burning underbrush to improve forest hunting grounds, mankind has tried to improve its environment, as beavers dam streams. We are experimental creatures working within the laws of nature. Our inventions that backfire, such as the Aswan dam or CFCs, are experiments that do not work successfully within those laws. The fact that we can neutralize our stockpiles of CFCs by using a substance found in rhubarb indicates the ongoing interaction between Schiller's and Fuller's natures. If we smile with pleasure at this solution, we reveal the value we put on Schiller's nature, and acknowledge a distinction between different kinds of "everything that exists physically." With this distinction we chide ourselves for our narcissistic preoccupation with those things we made ourselves over those things we didn't.

Progress is an evaluation of change. As technological change, the Aswan dam or CFCs are problematic; not progress, just change. But the term "progress" has come to be most commonly used in a propaganda sense, to endorse change, to sell it as inevitable. The distinction between change that is harmful and change that is not gets obliterated, and a suspicion of, or antipathy to change develops, replacing a prudently experimental attitude.

Schiller's nature, consisting of so many things we would never have conceived of inventing as well as things we find useful to us, remains a deep source of wonder. As such, even if it does not answer the question, What are we here for?, it nonetheless obviates the necessity of asking it.

Originally delivered at the symposium *Reinterpreting Landscape* at the Maier Museum of Art, Randolph-Macon Women's College, Lynchburg, Va., January 20, 1996. It is previously unpublished.

TITLES IN PRINT

EP 1 ALAN JONES, *Long After Hannibal Had Passed with Elephants. Poems and Epigrams.*

EP 2 BRUCE BENDERSON, *Toward the New Degeneracy. An Essay.* **(cultural criticism)**

EP 3 PETER HALLEY, *Recent Essays 1990-1996.* **(art)**

EP 4 NANNI CAGNONE, *The Book of Giving Back. A Poem.* **(Italian with English translation)**

EP 5 JONATHAN LASKER, *Complete Essays 1984-1998.* **(art)**

EP 6 CID CORMAN, *Tributary. Poems.* **With Beauford Delaney. (poetry and art)**

EP 7 B.H. FRIEDMAN, *Swimming Laps. Stories and Meditations.* **(fiction)**

EP 8 ABRAHAM DAVID CHRISTIAN, *La Salle des Pieds Perdus. Drawing / Zeichnung.* **(art)**

EP 9 REMO GUIDIERI, *Too Late Too Early. An Essay.* **(philosophy and aesthetics)**

EP 10 RACKSTRAW DOWNES, *In Relation to the Whole. Three Essays from Three Decades – 1973, 1981, 1996.* **(art)**